Cryptic Words.

By Srika

To someone who knows who they are,

I think I love you now.

Contents

Intro

Some things
Can be forever.

Even I don't know
Why I say that.
Please believe it to be true.

For me.

I have sat here
Day after day
Weaving my thoughts into songs,
Painting feelings on them,
Putting them together
Piece by
Piece.

Now all that's left
Is for me to sit back
And hope that you can read these poems
And find some meaning
Hidden
Deep within
These cryptic words.

Apple Straws

Let's play a game.

It's a game
That you can only ever win
Once in your lifetime.

First
Hear me,
Then answer my questions.

When I was born
I had opened my eyes for the first time,
But I can't remember it.
I can't remember what I saw,
Or what it felt like to discover sight.

I have grown now,
And it has been many years.
I have seen many many things
With these eyes of mine
But none of those things were beautiful.

At least until I saw my lover
For the very first time.

I still remember that,
And I cherish it with all my heart.

Now tell me,
If I could remember the very first time
That I opened my eyes,
Would I cherish that memory
More than the first memory of my lover?

Think about it for a while.
This question is important.
Choose your answer

After you're completely certain.

Next,

My mother told me
That I had learned to walk,
And then learned to run.

But nowadays
I do not walk
But simply run.

I cannot seem to slow down
Even when I try to.

I am always fast
Always moving quicker than I am comfortable,
And I fear that in my haste
I have lost something precious.

I feel the same way
About my lover.

I fear that every time we talk,
We move much too fast.
Before I could call them a friend
We are already tied together for life.

I have known no one but them,
And now,
I will never know anyone else.

Okay,
So answer my question:
Did I ever really learn to walk
Or was I born running from the womb?

For this one,
Don't think too much.
Tell me whatever answer

Comes naturally.

Next,

No one remembers
The first time they were happy,
But I know for certain
That once I met my lover
I have felt happy
Again and again.

Suddenly
Since I have known love,
All other emotions pale
To happiness
And I feel my heart sing with joy.

When I look at my lover,
And look into their eyes,
I think that they're happy as well.
They keep telling me
And re-assuring me
That they're happy.

Now for the question,
Tell me
Were either of us ever happy
Even once
Before meeting each other?

You know the answer
To this question.
No one can answer this question wrong.

And now,
I will ask you the final question.

I have talked of firsts
Again and again
Throughout this game.

Tell me if you know now,
Is my lover
The first lover I've ever had?

Have you answered?

Forget
All your answers.
It doesn't matter what you answered.
None of the questions held any points
In the first place.

Have you read this far?

Good.

By reading until this point
For the very first time
You have won.

You win
If this is the first time
You are reading this poem.

And now that you have won
You can never win again.

You will never get to experience this
For the first time
Ever again.

Your first is gone.

And you are forever changed by it.

To tell the truth,
I have not yet
Had my first love.

I do not have a lover.

Once my first is gone,
I will never get it back.

That makes me scared.

My first should be perfect
Because there are no do-overs
Is what I feel.

Maybe you feel
That way too.

Maybe your first
Has already happened
And you have now seen
That it isn't perfect.

But hear me.

Though you can never win,
You can always read this poem again
Anyway.

Of course,
You will lose.
It will not feel the same
As winning.

But maybe
Despite losing
You can find some deeper meaning.

Maybe you can read it
And think of your own firsts.

Maybe
You don't need to win
If winning means
That only your firsts matter.

So don't be scared.

Or I'll feel scared too.

If only firsts mattered,
Why would seconds exist?

Now,
Let's play another game.

This game
You can never win
In your lifetime.

You win the game
If you know why I named this poem
'Apple Straws'.

Shackles and Chains

1

The tall being bent down
Close to the surface of the water.

"Helpless," It whispered.
"Is this what helpless is?"

With a swish,
The surface erupted,
Water splashing
Spraying
Spritzing.

From that water,
A hand flew out
And reached.

A cry for help,
A desperate muffled scream,
A call for humanity,
As the hand's owner drowned.

But it was a pity,
For the being had no humanity to spare.

It was made of beginnings and ends,
Devoid of middles
It hopped from destination
To new destination
And the journey was long lost.

For such a being,
How could it understand?

How could it comprehend misery

When it had never laughed?
How could it comprehend death
When it had never lived?

"Well, if I give help,
It'll no longer be helpless."
The being nodded solemnly.

The hand went untouched
And slowly
Surely
It sunk back in.

"You can never escape from there."
The being told the hand
Or maybe it told the hand's owner.
"That's what you are made of.
You are made of confines,
Of physical barriers
Of shackles and chains
Forever rooted
To the same spot."

The water blew out bubbles.
The last breaths
Of the trapped soul
Flew upwards eagerly.
Even if the soul did not escape,
At least that little air did.

The being sat by the edge of the water.
"I am made of rivers.
I am made of water itself.
I bend and fold and meld
I swim
I float
And I can change to anything I desire."

The being thought to itself.
"These are simply facts.

Opinions don't belong to me,
And neither does personality.
I am nothing,
Because once I am something,
I will be bound
By confines, boundaries,
Shackles, chains,
And the rest."

The being realised that there was no point
In saying all this.
It stopped its conversation.

The water slowed.

The surface went still.

It was as if the lake's peace was never disturbed,
As if the incident hadn't happened.

The being continued to sit there,
Long after the soul was lost.

The being stayed quiet and simply watched.

The sun went about its day.
It sunk down,
And pulled the rest of the blue sky with it.

The being was met with a breeze
That was softly playing in the grass
And running between the trees.

The breeze grew violent
Until a large storm blew
And huffed
Over the being.

The rain came pouring down,
Like bullets,

Slapping hard against the being's head.

The being looked into the sky,
Letting the raindrops fall on its face.
It didn't flinch
And it didn't blink
Even when the drops hit its eyes.

When the being looked down at the water,
It saw a reflection.
An indication
That the air bore not nothing,
But an existence;
A something.

When it looked at the reflection
It saw its soaking wet self.
It saw the water dripping from its eyes.

It quite looked like it was crying.

How funny the winds were.

They painted emotion
On an unfeeling being.

"It was you, wasn't it?"
The being asked,
As it stared down.

Its voice was pleasant,
And it pulled its mouth into a smile
To signify that it bore no ill-will
To the wispy tendrils of air
That swished
And swooshed.

The wind roared appreciatively
Happy for acknowledgement.

"Who are you?"

Perhaps there was a reply,
But the being could not tell.
The rain went pouring on,
And the being was soaked wet.
The skies didn't reply with thunder or lightning.

Maybe this was silence.
Maybe
This was how rain communicated silence.

Or maybe
It was an answer in itself.

2

Drawing was fun.

A pastime
As old as time itself.

The being pulled on a long stick
And brandished it
Towards the soft dirt it sat on.

It used the stick
And drew lines in the soil,
Slowly,
Sketching its image in the dirt.

With the unpracticed
Squiggly lines of a child
And the same lack of limb coordination,
It drew a funny sketch
That nevertheless managed to describe it.

And then
With a sharp flick of the very limb
That had breathed life into the image
The being erased the picture.

Though the being could draw
As much as it wanted,
The end product could not be left to exist.
It would be destroyed.

For if it was left to exist,
It would say something of its creator.
The being would be either good
Or bad at drawing.
It would have opinions,
Styles and preferences.

That would define it.

What was more concerning
Was that it was a self portrait;
The most defining of things.

That would shackle it.

The being did not wish to be shackled.

Existence was the dread of all.

With a large laugh
The sky tickled it with wind.

The sky seemed to ask,
'Do you think I'm shackled?
I fly and float and grow.
I am the never-ending,
Ever-growing
Expanse.
I am beyond what you can think of.
I am beyond what you can be.

'If you wished to be what I am,
If finally you wished to define yourself
You could never become me.
That's what the shackles and chains do.
They make me unique
And unlike you.
They make me a someone
Who no one can be.
You, little being,
You are no one.'

The being scowled
And threw dirt at the air.

The air bristled.
The earth shook violently.

'Take not what is not yours.'
The trembling ground
Shaking the being
Seemed to say.

The earth shook in pain
As it stared at the uprooted ground.

The being
Sadly
Said out loud.
"But nothing is mine."

The sky whistled.
It whacked the being in the jaw.

Surprised and hurt
The being crawled onto
What would've been knees.
It sat and huffed
And stared back at the sky.
"I am nothing.
Nothing is mine.
Why whack me for that?"

Again,
The wind slapped the being
Right across its self,
Leaving an emptiness behind.

The being felt no pain,
However,
It felt the need for pain.
It felt an absence
Which should've been filled
With something
Anything.

Only then did the being realise

That the wind was playing with it.
It was being toyed with.

In silence
The being wanted to revolt.
But it held back,
For that would be a defining trait,
Would it not?

The being really did not wish
For definition.

3

The being sat by the water yet again.
It sat for days on end.
It watched the dancing water
Dip and jump
And spin round and round.

The sky grew impatient.
If it could speak,
It would've told the being,
'What are you waiting for?
Need you be so patient?'

The ground would've thumped.
'Patience is all one needs.
A way to supply everything.
Time will provide,
No matter what it be.'

The being heard them.
Its eyes didn't move from the water
As it spoke.
"No,"
The being said.
"This is not patience.
This is not impatience.
This is the absence of everything.
I have sat here so long
I had forgotten I was alive."

The sky was curious.
'Then why do you wake now?
If we have woken you
Do you have a presence
Instead of an absence now?
Have we somehow
Made you into something?'

The being thought in its brain.
As it mulled over the question
It fell asleep again.

After a few more days,
The sky seemed to stir it again.
'Wake.
Answer me.
Are you something
When you picture us talking?'
The earth silently listened in.

The being thought.
"I am still not present.
This is a chance;
An opportunity
For me to become something.
There are endless instances
Where I am given time to define myself."

'And yet you never use them.'
The sky mourned.

"And yet I never use them."
The being reaffirmed.

The ground quaked gently,
But it was enough to send the being flying.
'You are light.
You are able to be thrown.
You are that which has been sent flying.
Are these not definitions?'
The earth suggested.

The being frowned
And its face contorted in anger.

'Even your frown,
Your response,
Is enough to define you.'

The earth gently rumbled.

The being remained silent.
Instead of talking
It dug up chunks of earth and threw them
All around at random.

The ground trembled.
'Dare not
To touch what is precious to me
In your anger.
For my precious things are precious
And your anger is not.'

The being refused to listen
And threw handfuls of dirt in the air.

The sky then grew dark and heavy.
'Little one,
I love you,
But not when you're like this.'

The being bristled in fury.
"Love is unconditional.
It cannot be given
And taken
As you wish.
If you love me,
You do,
And if you don't,
You don't.
You do not wish me well
Despite your polite conversation.
Since we have met
You constantly question
Everything about me.
You have done nothing but try to define me."

'And you have done nothing but define all!
You define love

And get mad when it stretches beyond definition.
Understand that definitions
Are merely tools of understanding.
They bear no power over their objects.
Definitions of love can help you understand,
But just by saying nonsense
You can't make it true.
Definitions are just words in your head.
They cannot leave your head.'
The winds seemed to roar.

The being shriveled in on itself.
"You are cruel.
Wisdom is not cruelty.
Nothing wise can be painful."

'I thought you couldn't feel pain?'
The sky whispered.

The being refused to reply.

It went right back to watching the water.
It did not stir for many more months.

4

One day,
The ground swallowed the being up.

It opened wide,
Forming cracks in itself
Until there was a chasm.

With a gentle push
The being was sent rocketing in.
After a rough tumble
The being landed inside the hole.

The ground closed up the exit.

'Away from the sky,
I can say whatever I want to you.'
The earth said.

The being did not reply.
It laid still, like a limp doll.

'Answer me now.'
The earth rumbled.

Rocks fell from high.
The wet soil
Which was buried deep under the surface
Covered the being.
The chasm itself shook
As the self of the earth
Tried to shake out an answer
From the small, tiny being.

'Talk to me.
Wake up now.'
The earth growled.

"What is your question?"
The being murmured.

'Sit up first.'

"You really have no
Tact
Do you?"

The being sat up and stared at
The encompassing brown dirt
That sat above its head
Where the sky would normally be.
"You tell me,
Earth.
Why do you play at being sky?
Why do you hold me here?"

'If you have not yet began,
If you have not started to be,
That means that there's a beginning to existence.
Where there's a beginning
There will be an end.
Do I
The earth itself,
Have an end?
I cannot even recall
If I had ever started.
I cannot even recall
A time before being.
I had assumed I always was,
And I always will be.'

The being thought carefully.
"Why do you worry about ends?
It is not the end of the sky
Or the end of me,
But the end of you,
Yourself.
Just as you can't remember

Your start
You will not remember
Your end.
You will be beyond worries
So why waste time worrying about it now?"

The being heard a dull thud
And assumed the ground to be angry.

The ground shuffled.
'Ends are painful.
You would not understand.
For me to become nothing
Like you are now,
I would have to lose everything.
That is the pain
Of being a something.'

There was a louder thud.
Rocks fell
The ground cried out in pain.

The being looked up.
"Why are you in pain?
Why do this to yourself?"

With a loud sound
The ceiling broke into pieces.
The brilliant light of the sky
Pierced into the darkness,
It's bright blue tendrils
Lifting the being out of the hole.

With a gasp
The being found itself sitting
On the surface of the earth
Gazing up at that brilliant sky.

The sky seemed to rage.
'Take not what is not yours.

Do you recall those words?
The being beneath me
And above you
Is a being of sky
A child of the winds.'

'Claim not
What is not yours.'
The ground said angrily.

The sky retorted,
'There has never been any definition
For what is yours and what is mine.
For certain
The being does not belong to you.
Do not take it.'

The being gazed into the skies.
"I do not belong to you."
It felt that it should say the same
Again to the ground,
But for some reason
It did not.

Crack!
The sky broke in half
And threw winds
Rain
Hail
Misery
At the being and the earth.

The sky cried in betrayal.
'That dirty stamped ground!
The most sinful of beings.
It creates heedlessly
It is the parent of starts
It gives life to all
Without consideration
For the poor creatures who will now

Have to face their own ends.
Only now
It tortures and questions you
Because
Because
Finally,'
The sky laughed bitterly.
'It has realised its own end.
It knows of our mortality.
How prideful
To assume itself different
From the lives it makes and ends.'

The lightning and thunder
Drew bruises and burns
On the surface of the earth.

The sky continued.
'And you,
You being.
You are a fool to stand by it.
The earth fears the end
And you fear the start.
The both of you will remain in fear
Forever.'

The ground roared
And folded itself in.
The sky contorted to enwrap
The now bent ground.

The sky threw lightning
The ground spit rocks at the sky.
They clashed and
Clawed and
Clubbed each other in the head.

The being watched.
It was thrown
And tossed

Like a rag doll.
The sky and earth
Engaged in so fierce a battle
That it was indistinguishable
If the being was falling or flying.

It slumped over,
Mid-air.
What use had the being for all this?
It felt an awful lot like confines.
It felt like shackles.

The being did not like shackles.

Why had the being stirred in the first place?
It had been foolish to do.

It fell into a slumber
And would not move
Or speak
Or live
Anymore.

The sky quietly,
Sadly,
Watched it,
Even as it continued to lay strike upon strike
On the poor battered ground.

The sky,
If it could speak
Would've said,
'Why must you hide?'

The sky,
If it could speak
Would've said,
'Do I make you hide?'

The sky shrunk.

5

The being would not move.

The ground and sky nudged it.
'Wake.'
'Stir now, it has been long.'
'Are you still alive?'

In response to the last comment,
The sky told the ground
'It was never alive.'

The ground sighed.
'It was always alive.'

'That's not true.'

'Even now,
We cannot talk
Nor interact.
It imagines us interacting.
It imagines us into existence.
That we talk is proof
That the being is alive.
It has started.'

The being shifted uncomfortably
In its sleep.

The sky whispered.
'Don't make it mad.'

And so the being continued
To sleep.

The sky gently whispered.
'But I still don't understand
What makes the little being

So
So angry.'

The being did not respond.

The sky whispered,
'Little being,
You refuse to start
Because forever does not exist.
Think about that.
There is no forever.
Things won't always be the same way.
You have a chance now.
You can choose to exist.
You won't always have that chance.'

The being stirred.
"I wish for the day
When I am not offered
That which I hate."

The sky shimmered in joy.
'You are awake.'

The being huffed.
"I would rather be asleep."

The sky did not reply with words.
The winds hummed and sang a soft song
For the poor small being
That looked up at the bright expanse.

The ground did not speak
At all.

6

When the being looked up
It suddenly realised just how far
It had come.

Initially the being had sat by the lake
And then a different lake
And slowly
Surely
It had walked so far.

The being didn't know the way back.

"Sky,
Earth,
You both have watched me all this while
Have you not?
Please guide me home."

It waited for a reply
But instead found silence.

The sky rumbled
And rain started to pour again
After all this time.

The being called out.
“Please,
Take me back home.
I don’t want to be stuck here forever.”

Lightning struck.
It hit the ground
And blew a large blackened hole
Into existence.
The still alive tendrils
Of electricity

Whipped around
Painting spirals
Cracks
And glowing lines all along the ground.
The thunder resonated after a pause.

The being jumped away in shock.
It cried out,
“How dare you-”

The lightning struck again.
In fear
The being closed its mouth.
It hugged itself near
And prayed for the storm to disappear.

“Sky, Earth,
Sun, Moon,
Air, Water,
Life, Death,
Existence, Null,”
The being called out
In a small whisper.
“Come save me,
Come take me home.”

The storm refused to let up.
There was no shelter nearby.
The being simply rolled into a ball.

“The one who gave me existence,
The unnamed force,
The unnamed one who I love,
Please save me.
Please.
I wish for you.”

The wind howled.
The innocent, playful breeze was gone.
To think

That at one time even storms had been pleasant.
That felt
At least a small forever ago.

“Please save me.
I don’t enjoy suffering.
I am scared of pain.
I do feel it.
I pretend not to,
But I do.
Please come save me.”

Like a slap to its face
The rains hit the being
And pushed its face into the ground.

“Please save me.”
Its voice got louder.
“I despise fear.
It hurts to feel fear
I do feel it.
I pretend not to,
But I do.
Please come save me.”

The rain fell harder
On the being’s tired, weary head.
Its blood went cold
And its body shivered
As the storm continued above it

“Please save me.”
The being cried out,
Not even sure who it was calling out to.
“I really hate the cold.
It makes my body shiver.
I do feel it.
I pretend not to,
But I do.
Please come save me.”

In its desperation,
It couldn't control the words that came out.
"Please save me."
Its lips shivered.
"I really hate myself.
I fear I'm defined.
I do wonder about it.
I pretend not to,
But I do.
Please come save me."

It gasped as it heard
The words that had escaped.
They wouldn't stop.
"Please save me."
It felt tears stream down.
To think those winds
Would one day make it really cry.
The raw feeling
Left its face burning.
"I really feel scared.
I feel all alone.
I'm lost,
I'm in pain,
I'm in fear,
I'm cold,
I'm defined,
I have no hope left
For this world.
Will all of forever
Be spent in hidden suffering?
Will I never be alright?
Will I be lost and forgotten
And discarded
All my existence?
I had thought I could save myself.
I had thought I could live happily
If I ran from it all.
I had thought I'd be okay alone.

I had wished that I'd be alright.
I'm not.
I'm not alright.
Every day is spent in fear,
As I am pulled closer
Towards my ending.
Though I will one day end
And that day I will not worry
Every minute leading to it
Is spent with worries clouding my head.
When I look at my reflection
Or draw my image
I see a monster in place of me.
I watch as the supposed me
Swallows my hopes and dreams.
The flowers I hold
Wilt.
The water I touch
Dries.
The love I give
Dies.
If I am to live like this forever
Will I be given mercy in my next life?
Or will I be trapped again?
This life hasn't started yet
But it is already over.
I am broken
I cannot be fixed.
I am lost to all—"

And then the sky shattered.

With a roar,
The winds came to the being's rescue,
And blew the rain clouds backwards.

A wild flash of light
Lit up the clouds and the drops of rain,
Blowing them to smithereens.

The night sky was revealed
And the stars
Glowed dangerously bright
Behind the exploding lightning

And for a second the being saw
The fabric of its universe shake
And squirm
Beneath the immense powers of the sky.

The being stared in wonder
At what the sky was.
Was this the power of definition?

And then it was over,
And the clouds were gone.
The being was left staring
At the calm and still
Sky.

If it could talk,
The sky would've whispered,
'I have saved you.
I will guide you home.
I understand your pain.'

The being slowly nodded.
"Please,
Let's not talk about my pain.
I don't want to think about it."

The sky glittered
From the remains of the battle.
'You still have a chance.
You have admitted your faults
And all your pains.
You can exist now.
You can finally join us in existence.'

"I do not exist.

I never will."
The being frowned.
A tear fell
From its face.

It slowly stood up
And stared expectantly at the sky.

The sky would argue at this point.
It would talk of the pains.
It would call the being a coward.
Or at least that's what the being thought.

Wordlessly
The sky lit up the way home.

The being slowly followed it.

7

The lake showed no signs
Of the body that was once there.

The being slipped into the water
And swam to find the body.

It was not there.

The being wasn't exactly sure
Why it needed the body
In the first place.

It swam to the surface.

And sat there.

This time
It no longer was able to sit
For ages on end.
It was aware of every minute
And every second.
The being felt time
Pulling at it.

Maybe it was running out of chances.
Maybe forever was already over.

The sky and ground were quiet.

Could forever end?
The being wondered.

It ran its fingers through the water.
For the drowned body
Forever had already ended.

The being could've helped

But it didn't.

And now
Was the being itself
Finally helpless?

Helplessness
Felt worse than shackles and chains.
It felt like a cage.

The being felt itself shiver.

The sky seemed to smile.
'There is finally something
Much worse
Than existence.
But knowing you
That makes no difference at all.'

The being continued to run its fingers
In the cool water.

The sky said,
'To exist is not painful.
We fear death and ends
Because we fear not existing.
If that is true
Than we must fear
Not starting
Because that is also
Not existence.
But now
After all this time
If you still refuse to be something,
I will stop pestering you.
But know this:
Like you said,
Forever has already ended.'

The being hugged itself close.

The sky continued,
'If you are scared
Of what you will become once you exist
Don't think of that.
Think of what you want to become.
That is enough.'

The being felt another tear fall.

The sky said,
"This is your final chance."

There was a silence.

There was a pause.

There was a time when the being wondered
If it had the bravery
To face its fear.

The being whimpered,
And then pressed on a weak smile.
"I have existed all this time,
But now,
With a little courage,
I shall admit it."
It felt its hands go limp and weak.
But in a way
Its brain relaxed.
"I shall define myself."
Its heart tremored.
"I am scared of definitions
But I now have the strength
To overcome it.
I am scared of shackles and chains
But it will be alright
If I get used to them.
I am scared of being helpless
So I hope I now have help

And empathy.
And I wish to be alright
So that I can exist
And also be happy."

When the being was done
It looked into the sky for recognition.
It looked to the ground for appreciation.
But neither of them stirred.

Nothing changed about the world.

Being defined felt an awful lot
Like not being defined.

The being looked down at its hands
And saw them properly.
The being felt the physical ground
And acknowledged it.
It felt its heart beating
And acknowledged it.

It looked into the water
And saw not a monster
But itself.
The being was a strange creature
Once defined.

It was tall
And had horns
And had grey feathers.
It had always been hiding
In shadows and darkness.
It had been scared to look
At itself.

The being looked up at the sky.
"Are you there?"
It looked to the ground but didn't bother
To call out.

Once defined
The sky and ground
Never spoke to it again.

The being still continued to look up
And talk to the sky.

The winds ran around it joyfully.

The being said,
"I am now something.
What shall I be called?"

There was no reply.

The being smiled.
"I will call myself 'sky'."

It lied down,
And looked up.
"But why did you do this?
Why didn't you let me be?"

The gentle breeze blew
Once again.

"Has my forever finally started?"

My Colours are for You

I'll give you my colours

One by one

Oh how I love you
Oh how I wish to speak of love

I'm impatient for you
I wish to hold hands
I wish to run with you through the rest of my life

All my life is spent waiting for you
And longing for you

For understanding
And warmth
And love
And this feeling of your head on my shoulder

I know not of these things
I haven't yet even met you
I haven't become myself

But as I wait
I smile when I think of you
And I smile when I'm not thinking of you

The day will come one day
But till then the days are warm
And these days without you are numbered

I will come meet you at the doorstep
But I won't pick you up at the station

And the most important part is
You must enjoy the wait as well

Till then we sit far apart
With our hearts ever warm

I will love you
And I still do even now.

Burg with Gray Walls

I have nightmares
Somedays.

I close my eyes
And my breath goes cold.
I can feel the ice beneath my fingers.

In my dream
I see the tall buildings erupt out of the ground
And soar up high, high, high.

All the buildings
Are a cold merciless gray.

As am I.

I am gray.

As always,
I spend the first few minutes watching.
I stay quiet.
I duck behind a building
And I watch.

The city expands.

It expands constantly.
From the outer ring
To forever
It never stops.
The buildings keep sprouting
One after the other.
There is no limit
Or walls.

Every minute
As the city grows

My fingers get colder.

I shiver
And hide myself.

After I watch
And carefully ascertain
That there is no one else
I make a tiny move.

A foot of mine steps forward
Daintily
As if I walk over a frozen lake.

As always the whole city tilts.
The buildings lean forward
Just for a second
And then they adjust.

The city moves forward
So that it seems I am in the same spot.

I am clever.
I know I am moving.

It is like when a butterfly sits on a leaf
And you hold your hand beside it.
It then flies forward
And sits on a new leaf.
You move and again
Hold your hand beside the butterfly.

For the butterfly
It seems like it is in the same place.

But you know,
It has moved.

I take a few steps forward
And each time

The city shifts with me.
Every time I walk
I move the city
A significant distance from where
It had started.
Though I can see no difference
I have infinitely changed its path
And the outcome it produces.

Though it looks like the city
Has trapped me,
I now control it
And control where it goes.

Like how prey
Hold some power
Over their predators.

When the lion hunts for deer,
Momentarily
The deer has power over the lion.
The deer dictates
What the lion sees
What the lion does
And where the lion goes.
It can carry its predator
Through the forest
Down the hill
Or really wherever
It wishes to take the lion.

However
This power is useless
And a curse.

The deer owns power
Over the lion
Because the lion is vulnerable,
Hungry,
Greedy.

But this power cannot make
The deer strong
And those faults cannot make
The lion weak.

Ultimately
The lion takes back all the power
For soon the deer is dead.

The dead hold no power
Of their own.

I am stuck here.

I have no way out.

And these facts are true
Everytime
I have had this nightmare.

Now this is where it
Diverges.

Sometimes
I keep running
As far as I can,
Infinitely changing everything
And causing severe damage
To what this city
Would've been.

Sometimes
I go still again,
Watching and waiting
To see if the city has eyes.
I hide
In fear of the city that moves
And grows
For all of forever.

But never
Do I find why the city chases me.

The lion chases the deer
Because it is hungry.
It chases because it
Wants the deer and its flesh.
It chases to eat and kill
That scared little deer.

But I still don't know
What this gray city
Wants from me.

I stand tall
And straight
And look from here to there
In this cold
Uninhabited place.

What do I have
That this place needs?

I walk a small distance
Before I get tired.

The city is infinitely colder.
I am robbed of my willpower.

I feel it
On my back
On my chest
On my hands
My feet
My ears.
The city can see me.

It watches me.

It waits for me.

This time
The nightmare is different.

I can feel its greed
For the first time.

I step forward
And the city doesn't follow.

Immediately
I step back.

When the lion no longer chases
Behind the deer
There is only one explanation.

The lion is about to pounce.

This is the moment
Of the kill.

I stay in my place
Trying to remain calm,
Trying not to move.

Like the push to a pull
The waves of creation
Are met with
The waves of destruction.
The chill air
Turns hot.
It turns as hot as fire.
The once growing buildings
Tumble back down till
They lie in pieces
On the ground.
I wonder if I, too,
Will end up the same.

But fear not for me.
Don't feel sad
Or grieved.
What grows
Falls
What falls
Grows.
So there is no emotion needed
When something
Falls or grows.

Did you believe that?

You fool.

There is no pain
Or pleasure
In life or death.
They are both paid for
In currencies beyond you and me.
There is no sorrow
Or joy,
But there is un-sorrow
And un-joy.
And those extreme emotions
Are felt by the whole universe.
There are so many
To share it between
That you end up with only a fragment.
That fragment
Is so so small
That you barely feel it.
You do not understand it,
And never will,
Unless you learn to feel the emotions
And opinions
And thoughts
Of everyone
Who has ever existed
And will ever exist

In all time.
That is the big picture
You speak of.
That is the real truth
That you need to understand.
You need to have seen
Every side
Every angle
To really feel the emotions
That only gods can feel.

I cannot feel that way.
I end up
Feeling fear.

I suddenly remember
That I have chosen to come here.

Was this not just a dream?

I struggle
To wake,
To leave this world behind.

But nightmares
Cannot be woke from,
And problems
Cannot be solved by thinking,
Or else who would
Have nightmares or problems?

The city
Tumbles
As I watch it fall
And I am stuck here
And trapped.

Why do I get stuck?

Why do I have fear?

Why do these buildings
Only ever make me sad?

There's a light
And there's a very small fire
Right there
In the corner of my eye.

I have stumbled upon it.

I have chanced upon why
This city
Troubles me every other night.

I have found
The source of its greed.

It's me.
It is simply me
And all that I am.

The nightmare wants me.
It wants me to give my essence of being
All away to it.

That is too heavy a cost
To give away
Because of a moment of fear.

It is too heavy a cost
Even if
I won't be really giving it away.

After all,
This is a nightmare.
Once I wake up
This'll all cease to exist
And I will own myself again.

Maybe
Once I give myself up
The nightmare will be over
And I will wake up
As I have completed it.

But it's too heavy a cost
And my heart will not let me
Give up anything I hold dear
Even in dreams.

I must cover myself in trinkets
And hold close anything
That makes me feel safe, happy, alive.

But like the creation waves
Have destruction waves
And how the un-sorrow
Has un-joy
For my happiness,
There will be a price to pay someday.

But listen,
I have had a hard time.
I am trapped in a nightmare
I am trapped in a city
I am trapped in my own beating heart.

Just as how I fell asleep
I will sometime inevitably
Have to wake up.

But listen,
Universe.
Listen to me,
All of you.

Just this once,
Won't you pay the price for me?

Won't you let me be happy,
Without having to make me sad?

Won't you tips the scales,
And disobey nature
Just this once
Because I beg you?

Please don't make me repay my debt
Because then
For my life of happiness
I will have to pay with my being.
I have taken too much
And now I owe
My everything.

Let the scales tip.

Let the push lose its pull.

Even if it means
That I will never wake from this nightmare,
Save me from what I've done.

Let me sit here forever
Frozen in my slumber,
The gray city around me
In a state of half-creation half-destruction
Whiling away my time
Until time itself ceases
But still
Always
Completely
Happy.

Happy
Without consequences.

My love,
My Universe,

My everything,

I wish you
Goodnight forever.

The city winks out of existence
And I am left in a null,
Slowly
Even my words
Start to dissape—

Heart of Silver Light

My heart has been ripped out
From my chest.
I watch it struggle to beat
As shards of glass
Pierce through it.
I look to the moon and cry,
“What did I do to deserve this?”
I scoop it into my arms
And wrap it in white cloth.

I jump from rooftop
To rooftop,
Holding my heart,
Whispering to it
That I will save it.

What's left of my hope
Gathers all around,
Like a veil,
Shielding me from
The long slim eyes
That watch me from the dark.
I really love
That feeling
of protection.
I really wish
For that feeling.

I got cheated today.

That which was precious
Was robbed from my unspeaking body.
And then I felt the pain.
The guilt I felt from that
Was immense.

Because I have now

Been taught pain,
The smallest scratch
Reminds me of how it felt
To be ripped open
And clawed
From the inside

I cradle my heart
And stop to check
If it still beats.

Thump
Thump
Thump

It still holds life.
It holds all that I am.

I tell it I will save it.
I look into the skies and cry,
"Save me,
From this wretched place,"
That moon
Can it hear me?
If it could listen
Would it help me?
I give out a mirthless laugh
And stifle my tears.

I jump to the next rooftop.

The assaulters must be close.
They sliced
And cut
And chopped my veins up,
Not allowing my heart to work
Not allowing my blood to flow.

They raised a glass to me,
Praised me,

Held me close,
And then dropped the glass
On my
Fragile fragile heart.

Even now
My heart is quaking.
It begs for a release
From this dark cruel pain.
It begs for a reason
For this dark cruel pain.

I sense a stillness in my heart.
I quickly press two fingers to its side,
Gentle enough to not harm it,
Firm enough to still its fears.

I rock it side to side
And whisper reassurances
As I check its pulse.

Thump

Thump

It's slower than before.
Has it calmed?

I feel a shiver on my back
And whisk around
Eyeing the dark figures
Who chase me through the night.

What's left of my heart
Trembles.
It's definitely not calm.
Why has its pace slowed?
Is it dying?

What little courage

Is left in these butchered veins
I gather and pull into a long blade.

I grab and spin and throw,
Nailing an assailant in the chest,
But when I see the blade pierce
It feels as though my own chest
Is the one being stabbed.

Thump

My heart barely moves.
I sit down on the rooftop,
And hurriedly tighten the wrapped cloth,
My hands shaking.

I tell it that it's all okay.
I will save it.
I won't let it die.
As I bandage the
Feeble feeble heart,
I look to that cruel moon
And beg it to help.
I beg for it to rescue me
And my
Poor poor heart.

Thump

My heart spouts blood
One last time
Before turning into a spluttering mess.
I feel my vision go dizzy
And my death grow near
Just as my heart gives up.

The lump of flesh
Now slowly turns still.
I cradle it,
Hug it.

No longer scared of hurting it,
I really hug it hard.
I feel the glass press into
My arms and chest
And the sorrow
Seep into my bones.

Is this my end?
Is this all I get?
I have never wronged anyone.
Yet why does my fate hold this for me?

The moon remains up there
As impassive as ever
Even as my life finally leaves me.
I should be angry
Or upset,
But what do trivial things
Like that matter?
I smile back.

My eyes close
And death's warm fingers greet me,

And I feel safe finally.

THUMP

My eyes flutter open for a second
As I am momentarily
Given life again.

I see the butchered mess in front of me.
I pass away again.

The silence conquers all my senses,
Leaving me to feel numb
And poisoned.

THUMP

I gasp a breath of air.
My skin tingles from the brush of life.
My body sits up in alarm.

My hands automatically clench
And end up crushing the remains
Of my dear dear heart.

Shakily,
I look around at my surroundings
Before I fall back again
And pass out.

THUMP
THUMP
THUMP

I sit up
And grab my neck
As I physically feel
My veins brimming with warmth.
In a daze,
I stand
And take a shaky step forward.

The blood within me burns
With an aggressive silver glow.

My ears are blinded
By the heated heartbeat that fills my ears.

I look down at the ground
And see my dead heart.
How am I awake?
How am I alive?

Sharp pain shoots through me
And my neck snaps upwards

To face the large sky.

The moon is so close to the earth
That I feel its presence
Pulling me towards it.
It's so big
I can barely see the rest of the sky.
I feel its aura
Pierce through me.

And I see it pulsing
And giving me energy
And giving me life.

It pumped
As if it were my own heart;
It moved for me
And me alone.

I stared in shock.
I pressed my hand over my chest
And felt the moon itself
In that gap.

Slowly,
A timid
Weary smile
Rests on my face for a moment
Before I hurriedly get rid of it.

It feels bad and unnatural to smile.

I collapse to my knees
And find my arms holding
The flesh that was once my heart.

I hold it close
And whisper silent apologies
That I could not save it.

I cry.

I cry to the moon,
"I couldn't save my heart."

It continues to beat steadily
Unaffected by emotions.

"I couldn't even save my own heart,"
I curl into a heap on the ground
And stare up at the sky.

I watch my heart of silver light
Glowing dangerously bright
In the dark sky
As it protects me
And sends sleep into my bones.

I grow tired
And feel my eyes slowly close.

Before they can close
And fall into slumber,
I whisper to the moon,
"But you were able to protect me.
You saved me.
Thank you.
I love you."

In that moment
The world around me shifts
To show anything and everything
Beating
As my heart.

The trees beat,
The stars beat,
The buildings beat,
The night beats,
The ground I'm lying on

Starts to beat.

Surrounded by more hearts
Than I can count
I press another tired smile on.

“I feel safe.”

Malar-ing

1

The world is cold.

From where I come from,
There is nothing.
Even I myself didn't exist there.

The very first moment I appeared
And stood here
On this world,
I felt the chills run down my bones,
My limbs frozen in fear
Before the grandeur of existence.

But life,
Life itself is warm.

We all have memories
Of the time we couldn't remember.
Even if you can't remember anything else
You remember it was warm,
It was safe,
It was yours.

And the heartbeat in our veins
Is the last remnant
Of that feeling

A small echo of what we used to be.
A reminder
That there are things beyond us.

I still think about how
This warmth keeps me going.
It makes me wonder how much more

I had been 'going'
Back when everything was warm;
When everything was alive.

For the first few moments
Existence had been peaceful.
I was not yet wholly part
Of the world
And everything had been
So still,

Still,

Still,

Sudden!

In a clamber
The trees had groaned
And the soft ground had fallen apart
Under my feet.
My back had hit something hard
And all of existence had suddenly
Sprung to life.

I was given eyes
So I opened them for the first time
Only to see the angry sun.

With a yelp I fell back.

And then I saw her.

When the light left my eyes
I saw a girl staring at me,
Tears pouring out.
The light danced on her skin
And her tears glimmered as they ran down her face,
The sparkling light making them look like
Falling stars

Tumbling from the sky.

My senses were focused on her
As the rumble of life
Showed me the face of another,
A someone
For me to meet for the first time.

“Please leave,” she had cried.
Her voice had left me trembling;
It was something else I remembered
From the time before existence.

“I don’t need you here,” She insisted,
And suddenly looked down,
Too cowardly to look up.

I reached for my voice
But I did not have one yet,
So I watched her cry in silence.

“I’m not that lonely.”
She gasped between sobs.
My forming vocal chords had begun to creak.
“I don’t need to imagine.
I already have friends.”
She hugged her arms.

I opened my mouth to speak,
finally with a voice,
But she yelled,
“Leave!
You're just a figment of my imagination.”

And then she stopped thinking about me.

I disappeared.

2

I woke again.

This time it all happened
So so fast.

In a few seconds,
I was standing there,
As real as ever.

"Here," she thrust a cup of tea forward.
Her thickly lined eyes scrutinised me,
As I lifted the warm brown liquid
To my pink lips
To pretend to take a sip.

And then she changed her mind.
I lifted the cup to my
Now red lips.

There's something scary about having someone
Control you with their thoughts alone.

Her name was Jasmine,
No- it was Malar.

I set the cup on the table again.
"Malar, your friends don't love you."

It hurt me a little
To find that most could only speak
In this dreadful way.

Even in the depth of her mind
Where no one could see
She was still scared to speak the truth.
She needed me to say it.

Is that really alright?

Malar stared at her fingers for a little while more.
"I think they're just a bit busy these days.
They don't have enough time for me."

I sighed. "They have time.
They're just jerks."

"No," She insisted.
"I should give them another chance."

"There are plenty of others who care for you,"
I started,
But then I saw the hurt in her eyes.

I realised why.
The reason why I was there,
Was because she didn't have others.

There was a short silence.
I watched the gentle breeze
Brush her hair,
The sun inviting her to play
But she remained in her place,
Silent.

Anything was better than silence.

I hurriedly started talking.
"Don't you like dancing?"
She loved dancing.
I loved dancing.

I stood up.
Maybe we could-

I don't like dancing.
I sat down.

“Your friends don’t deserve you.”
I told her as I sipped my tea.
“You need to move on,
And focus on getting new friends.
You’ve tried your best to get them to like you,
But-" I struggled to finish.
"But it isn’t working.”

She nodded and finished her own tea.
She looked thoughtful,
As if my words had affected her.
As if they weren’t her own words.

I looked down at my own tea cup.
It was still full.

As someone who wasn’t real,
It was obvious that I couldn’t drink it.
I can’t drink.
I can’t eat.
I can’t touch real objects.
I can’t exist in places without Malar.

Still,
At that moment
Something made me do it.
I lifted the cup up.

I pushed the cup to my lips and tilted the glass,
Ready to take a sip,
But by then she was done,
And I was no longer needed,
And so no longer existed.

I disappeared.

3

She isn't here right now.

I've put out the lights
And hidden the house.
No one will stumble upon us.

Can you hear it?
How the soft hum fills the air?

The stars come out to play
In the crazed darkness
But only if you wait enough.

I digress.
Sit here for a while.

This reminds me of a time.
Once,
I had met with someone like this.
They had told me that
We weren't connected by fate
Or destiny
Or anything like that.

The thought that we would find each other
Again
In the vast universe
Was comforting
But false.

They told me
That the only things to connect us
Were memory
And our own desire to meet again.
Nothing more.

When did I meet them?

Um.

Forget I said anything.

I called you here
For something else.
We need to talk.

Before we continue with my story,
You need to understand two things
If you are to make any sense of what is to come.

First,

The bird who prepared
And spent time learning how to fly
Fell when it finally stepped into the sky.

Despite all its effort
It fell to its death.

The bird who didn't prepare
And stepped into the sky
Fell just like the previous one.

The third bird fell as well
But the fourth flew.

Out of the two deer
The lion killed one
But let the other one go.

It rained in one city
But didn't in the one beside it.

One flower wilted
But the other one bloomed.

You can hear me now
But she can't.

I was imagination
But she wasn't.

And now for the second thing you need to understand:

I am a liar.

4

As it turned out
Despite most of her friends snubbing her,
Malar did have a good friend.

I followed her down the narrow street
As she walked to her friend's house.

Step-step-halt-step
Cried her nervous footsteps.
How nerve-wrackingly slow we walked.

The dark was spreading through the sky
Glowing and growing
The colour of black, blue and brown
Seeping through the skies into Malar's mind.

"Why are you here?" she finally asked me.
"I'm doing fine on my own,
I don't need you right now."

I didn't know why I was there either.
"You're the one who's thinking of me."
I told her.

The sky changed its colours
And faded to a darker shade of almost black.
I stared up at it.

We climbed onto the uneven sidewalk together.
Though it seemed off,
"Are you nervous?"
I wondered out loud.

She didn't reply.

So she *was* nervous.

“Go away,
Disappear.
I’ll be fine on my own.”

I turned to her.
“So stop thinking of me.”

Like a gust of wind
I felt her mind press in on me,
Folding me like paper
Until I was bent like origami
No longer sure which side of me was up or down.

As I was pushed,
There was a foothold
For me to hold onto.

A place to stand
And push back.

I let my foot slip over it,
Choosing to be blown away.

It was too soon to push back.

5

I was gone for quite some time.

I thought she wouldn't need me again,
But she called on me
As the evening drew to a close.

My eyesight was hazy and
I felt warm all over.

I was there for a second
But the moment I appeared,
I saw her friend.

And then,
Her friend saw me.

But then again,
It was probably a trick of the eyes.

I only mention it
Because,
Well—

6

Like in a small cocoon
I feel warm
Almost all the time.

But when I see you,
My heart goes cold.

7

The sound of my heart racing woke me up.

The soft sound was louder now.

Where was Malar?
Where was I?
The ground was cold and hard.

No,
This place wasn't meant for me.

The gray filled my vision,
And my eyes were lined with silver.
Coins rained from up high,
The metal on their surface rusting brown.

My hands reached for support
But all is mist
In a world your mind can't control.

For if you can't hold the reigns
Someone else will.

Through the dark grey build
Of the ever widening sky
I saw a horse
And I saw myself
And I saw so much
And I did not wish to see.

I closed my eyes and wished
I would disappear.

And so I did.

8

When I met Malar again
I did not know her.

I never knew her well,
But I felt that I didn't know her at all.

No wait,
I think that I did know her well?

By this time
The timelines were mixed
The story was wrong

So I could only
Comfort myself with lies.

"Malar,
Why do I exist?"
I asked her.

She smiled.
"Because of me."

No, that's not right.
I erased the question and did it again.

"Malar,
Why do I exist?"
I asked her.

She thought about it.
"Are you sure you exist?"

Existence
Is not what is in the real world.

Anything and everything exists
Even if just within your mind.
For your mind
Is part
Of everything
And everything
Is existence.

Still,
It was wrong.
I did it again.

"Malar,
What if you don't exist?"
I asked her.

And poor soul,
She couldn't reply to that.

She was left speechless
And her mind took over.

Once again,
As all the previous times,

I disappeared.

9

Of things unordinary
Of things I haven't seen
I can't tell you about,

So know that though I lie
I have seen all this.

But what if I have seen
Everything?

I know all the faces here
And all is familiar,
But the only face here is yours
And it's staring back at me.

I can know all
If all is not much.

The palm trees swayed
For yet another night.

The night grew wide
To welcome the sway of its trees.

"Listen."
I said.
"Please listen."

And beside me was not Malar
But you.

And you heard me.

You walked beside me
As I walked forward.
Our feet made marks in the sand

Beside each other.

The crooked trees bent,
Forming shapes in the dark
Until they looked like
Our intertwined arms.

Ahead was darkness.
Behind was light so bright.

I turned to look back
And the light burned my eyes.

We stepped into the water
And the footsteps left on the pond
Sent waves towards the light.

Burnt by the glow,
The pond water turned into
Clouds of transparent ash.
The rearing waves
Lowered their peaks in fear
And the fish didn't stray that far ever again.

I stopped
And stood
And kept my eyes open.

After watching it all unmoving,
I finally closed my eyes.

Then all was dark.

I disappeared.

10

Sunlight and moon combined
To make the sweet hum
Belonging to silver and gold strands of light.
They weaved through the window.

I turned to Malar.
"People forget fast,
Don't they?
You're going to forget me."

She didn't deny it.

I continued.
"So if one day I forgot you
Would you forgive me?"

She didn't reply to it.

Why would she?
I was a small part of her
Owned by her mind.
She didn't need to listen to me.

But if I was controlled by her,
And she didn't want to hear,
Why would I ask
In the first place?

"Have you already forgotten me?"
I asked.

She didn't tell me to leave.
She didn't dismiss me.

She stopped thinking of me.

I didn’t disappear.

She saw me
And panicked.

I didn’t disappear.

Her mind tried to flush me out.

I didn’t disappear.

I stood so close to her
That she could feel the presence
Of existence itself
In me standing there
As real as she was.

I wouldn’t disappear.

"One day I will forget you," I told her,
My steps bringing me closer.

She backed away,
Suddenly scared
As if we weren't part of each other.

Her tears rained down;
The ebb of light lost;
The broken dying stars
Winking out.

And I had done this to myself.
I was still doing it.

"So forgive me when I don't remember your name,"
I whispered,
All warmth belonging to me in the moment.

I felt pity,
For one who I am one with.

"But whatever will happen then,"
I held her hand,
Pulling her close,
Her body like an empty shell,
My eyes revealing the null inside her.

I made her look at me.
Her wide eyes held nothing inside.

Through them,
Those empty eyes,
That empty soul,
I found it again;
The warmth from all those years ago
From before time began
From the place I've searched for all this time
From where I don't remember.

I found the warmth that was once mine.

"For now, I still remember you
And think of you
As if you were me myself."

And I let her go.

She disappeared.

11

"You're an imagination."

"Then why do I feel alive?"

"Because I imagined you to be alive."

When she didn't believe me,
I told her again
"Malar, you're imagination."

As I said,
I'm a liar.

As I said,
The world makes no distinction.
It assigns hot and cold
Life and death
Existence and void
At utter random.

"Why?"
Her voice was vulnerable,
Soft
In its heartbreak.
"Why make me think I was real?
Why make me think you weren't?
Why are you making me cry right now?"
Her tears rolled again.

"Because once a lion killed a deer
And let the other one go." I told her.

But I shall tell you the truth.
Why were you and I made?

You need another reason?

Very well.

There were never any deer to begin with
So it was fine
When the lion killed one.

12

You've come to see me?

The light is blue, brown and black.
The light is black.

I don't want to see you.
Please leave.

You're not leaving?

That's why I'm scared of you.

I can't make you cry.
I can't make you believe me.
I can't make you disappear.

Do you want to know who I am?

I'll show you.

13

Close your eyes.

Open them.

A small blue room,
A person,
A table,
A chair,
And above it all,
A yellow light on the verge of going out.

That's all I am.

Now leave.
Disappear.

14

My voice is still my own.

I can’t make you disappear
But I can make myself disappear.

Sit with me again.

Watch the stars
Fly through the world.

Look at the stars I've caught.

The palm trees
The night
The sun and moon
Are just like that time.

Isn't it great?

We've found each other again after all this time.

We're each other's connecting strings.

And I've finally told you the truth.

All of it.

Even the truth I wouldn't tell you in our past life.

And finally

Finally

After all this time

I am free from my burdens.

I will always remember you,
Jasmine.

You can finally believe me.

15

But then again,
I'm still a liar.

Colourless Self

This world is colourless.
It was always that way, huh?
Funny how you act like it was always dark.
Wasn't it different?
You're so cute.
You're so soft.

Forget that.
Cuter is how you hold my hand.

Drag me closer
Push me farther
Spin me around
Anyway, I'll always be here.

My feet hurt.
Don't spin me anymore.
I shall stay where I am.

I am drained of colour.

You're still here?
But you left.
That wasn't you?

You won't leave?
You will?
You hate me?
You can't tell me?

Close your eyes and sleep.
I don't wish to know your mind
Or you, yourself.
This is far enough.
Fare well.

Song of Nightmares

Deep within
Far from where I can see,
They lurk.

Behind every coral
Beneath every hull
Sunken like the hopes
Of those they drown,
They wait.

They exist only here
In this sea
When I'm afraid.

Their song,
Their cries,
Their smooth slippery voices.

They'll feed me lies about who I am
And who they are.
They'll feed me lies about
Who I love.

I shouldn't listen to their songs
Or they'll steal my ears away.

I shouldn't rhyme or they'll claim my life
And leave me dead to the world.

I shouldn't fall into the rhythm

I shouldn't fall into you

I know this.
I know this *but*—

I can see the
Black wave
Crunching on me
I hold your face
And whisper slowly.

The song lulls me
And puts my mind to sleep.
I try to wake
But its slumber's deep.

My lips; they move
To the lyrics I hate.
Something I can't
Even begin to say.

I speak:
"Please stay forever."

The wind is picking
And raising a storm.
I'm scared to stay inside
Cause inside is warm.
I'm scared to be where I am
Because it's always hard.

No.
I hold myself.

I'm listening to your song.

You're feeding me lies.

I am not myself
When I sing your song.

But I've grown over pain
I've taken a knife.
I've held your hand
In the darkest of nights

I write to you often
But you never write back
It's the reason I reckon
That you'll love me to death
Once I'm dead
And gone
And lost
And poisoned
And killed in your song of nightmares.

I shake myself
And stop myself
From falling deeper.

This pitiless sky
Is not my home,
And your wretched self
I have never loved.

I don't know you.

You are a part of this sea,
Slippery siren. You are
Someone I have never seen.
With a throw of
A rod,
Like a fish
I could catch you.

But somewhere, I hear

I *hear*

The soft cry of the moon
As the stars swoop in
The glint in its eyes
As its glow fades dim

The cry of the birth
Of the moonlit child.

The crazy desertion
The wild in your smile.

I stay in the moment
And hold on tight
As the sky clambers
And I cry out in fright
The sound of the waves
Hit my body in time
For me to see your face
*And speak again in rhy*me

No.
I won't.

I won't rhyme.

I am already wet,
And soaked in this salt water.

I have to stay strong.

Your face grows sad.
You *want me to rhyme?*

I never could bear to see you sad.

Follow pain into darkness
Is what they all say
To try to give in now
Is harder than sane
I'm scared to be alone now
And my hands have gone cold
Just give me your heart now
Before we get old
We've fought over mountains
Time has yet to claim
The fame for the moment
The shot that I aim
Cause if I steal into you

And pull you in tight
Will you give in to me?
Or will you leave me tonight?

Please stay forever.

Strings are broken
Light goes dark
No more rhyming.

I don't want to say another word.

Fools.

The lot of us.

The sea breaks the boat.
I am thrown into the water.

My arm's broken
My eye's broken
My heart's broken
My leg's broken
My stomach's broken
My heart's broken
My rib's broken
My bone's broken
My heart's broken
My toe's broken
My ear's broken
My heart's broken
My hand's broken
My heart's broken
My heart's broken
My heart's broken
My heart's broken
My heart's broken
My heart's broken.

But water it with milk

And drown in radiance
The birth of a new self
That belongs
Above
Higher
Happier
Healthier.

Swish,
The dress goes
Flow,
The river cries.

And for tonight
Death has died.

The silly nurture
The silly hope
Has lost its face now
It cries and gropes.
The rising sun
Shows me the day
And I wish to hold you
And someday I may
Apologise for the deeds
And crimes I've done
But now we hold again
Underneath the sun
Bequeath me with love
And a kiss on my hand
I'll never forget you
Or who I now am.
Shoot me in the head
Until I wake up again
Whisper to me sweetly
As the milk turns to rain.

Please stay forever.

I'll join you where forever is given abundantly.

Even if I am dead to the world
I will forever be with you.

Maybe there,
In the drowned darkness
We will be together
Like we used to be.

Pull the veil over
Dock the ship
Fade the lights colour
My heart will rip
I sing to you now
Because of fear
I give to you now
All I hold dear
Now sing to me
At least one time
Before the clock
Tolls it's last chime
Ring it out
And call my name
It's too far now
I'm not the same
Please write me back
Before you leave
I'll leave my heart
So it doesn't grieve
Don't fade now
Don't leave me alone
I wanted all time
But that's no time at all
If I cry out in curse
Will you stay by my side
How cruel is your game
For my pain to subside
With just a flick
And a flicker of hope
I wish for you now

I cling to the rope.

No time
Is all time.

Did I ever exist at all?
Was I really once alive?

All I remember
*Is the water all ar*ound me,
The sunken ship,
And this horrid pain in my chest.

I cannot tell
If I am wounded
Or if *I miss you.*

Why didn't you stay forever?

Sitting Alone

As I sit here alone
I realize that I think of you sometimes.

I sit by myself
And I think.

I always think when I shouldn't.

I think of holding your hand and knowing you
And running through the night by your side.
I think of what I've never seen,
I think of what we mean when we smile.

I've lived so many lives and been through this so many times.
I've seen you cry and hold me.
I've seen you push me away.

All the lives that have been lived before us
Are yours and mine now.
We are now standing in the spotlight;
The time has finally come.

I've waited long for this and even time itself has been generous
By giving me this time with you.

But all the world's stories
All the world's love and laughter
The sorrow and joy
Hold no meaning in this center stage.

I think about those who are so wrapped up in themselves;
They never see the bigger picture.
I think about the countless people
Who have held hands here
Just like you and me.

I think of the people who have loved
And lost each other in the sea of space and time,
Like distant stars who appear to stand together
But suddenly seem lonely when you block out one
With the palm of your hand.

As I continue to sit here
Alone
I think of how distant we are now.
But by thinking of you
I come a little closer to you—
Just a footstep or two closer.

I can feel the cold wind blowing through my hair.
As I reminisce I can see the ever moving stars.
It's night but it's not really that dark,
And the sky is a deep blue.
My hands are in your hair
Your face is against mine
And the chill that runs down my back is because of you
And I tell you I love you
As I do now.
I swear to protect you
By giving not my life,
But the very life force that flows through everyone
That has painted so many pictures.
I will protect you
Even if I have to give up the promise of time
And the promise of something after death.

As I decide I no longer want to sit alone,
I try my best not to think
Of how that day your eyes had held me,
Of that expression on your face.

I try not to think of how
You had promised to protect me too.

The House of the Night Itself

We will never escape the night.
I was once sure, but I was proven wrong that
We are safe here.

Pain in my heart
And
Pain in my eyes.
There is no longer
Hope that we will be alright.
I know that there is
Only one outcome to this night.

I had thought that there would be
Solace in this abandoned house.
There is
A great monster living in the walls.

We can defeat
Anything but this.
We'll fail to survive because of
Weakness.
We have no
Hope left.
There's
Thousands of things
I needed to tell you.

Initially
The house had been filled with light.
There was trust in my heart.
And then
I heard a quiet whisper.
And then
There was a loud rumble.

Suddenly,

The house was filled with darkness.
I cried out in fright.
You grabbed my hand.

A shimmer of sorcery wrapped around you.
I wondered what was happening.
Your eyes fluttering,
I looked at you.
You groaned
And then
You were still.
I saw
Then
Your lifeless body.
I looked at you,
And I cried
And I cried
And I cried.

It was so sudden.
Your death,
It made no sense.
This evil place,
I was trapped in.

I yelled out terribly.
"Please come back.
Come back to me, please.
Reverse time if you have to!
I need you beside me forever."

(Read from bottom to top)

Transcendence

Does music transcend soul?
Does life transcend death?

In another world I am born again to see their moonlight
But all moonlight is mine
For my fingertips to experience something foreign
Is what I dream for,
Yet it draws near
To my distance

If I count my breaths
Would I breathe faster or slower?
The sounds of my sleep
The heart of mine that isn't nearly loud enough
Maybe in my mind we're all different.

You for the first time draw nearer
Maybe something gentle is born
Maybe something soft is created
Maybe you and I will find it there
Maybe these maybes don't mean a thing to you now
Maybe there's no meaning that exists
But I want to search for meaning anyway.

Can I hold on to you?
These words are never enough
I was taught these words by someone else
And so when I talk I just repeat what they taught me
Am I not original?

They weren't original either
When I learn to talk I learn that
Good is good
And that
Bad is bad
What does that mean?
Will

Good be good
And will
Bad be bad
For the rest of my life?

You have to let go to understand this desperate cry.
Though I have mentioned my words failing me
Though I have ripped myself apart in these symbols
That I draw and call 'letters'
I still weave my message through this song of lies

My tongue can never grasp the right tunnel of air.
Underneath my feet, the ground gives way
And my head concocts a million reasons why
My palm is to be held to me and me alone.

But then why does it reach outwards?
Why give it the choice to reach outwards?
Were we born with our arms spread outwards?

Maybe if my head wasn't so heavy I'd be talking sane
Then again if I were to be any more light headed
The thoughts wouldn't form
And would be left like the cold tendrils of a small sapling
Sad and alone,
Curling in on itself
Because it cannot reach outwards
And never will
No matter how hard it tries

Will you hold my hand?
Will you scoop me up?
If you won't,
I will.
I will hold your hand.
I will scoop you up.

And what of entropy?
Do we all walk towards the edge?
Will everything we do fail?

Is everything made to break?

Do we all walk towards the edge for a reason?
Will everything we do fail in order to put away hurt?
Is everything made to break because we were perhaps
made to be single atoms and not matter?

Will I find it all there?

In the chaos I'll turmoil
And we'll stay in turmoil
Until one day there is nothing left.
When everything is destroyed
When there's nothing left to crumble,
The world won't be there.
Existence will be forced into stagnancy.
In that stagnant universe
Will I find something new?
When it's all gone
What will be left?

If all nature shows me the path to destruction
Why am I scared to follow?
One day I want to see that sight
But until then I'll take my time.

Because
If in the end,
Everything falls,
If the world will one day stop spinning,
Why did it spin in the first place?
Is it wrong
And naive
And childish
To wish it to spin forever?
Is it wrong
To be scared?

Until then,
I'll show you what the wings on my back

Look like on the ground.

I'll show you what my crown looks like
When it is shattered into pieces
As small as my fingernails.

I'll show you everything that I have ever touched,
Broken, destroyed and utterly defeated
By the forces of this world.

And then I'll move aside and show you the distance I have flown

I'll show you the land I've reigned over

I'll show you all my life
And all I've done
And all I've shaped this world to be.

I'll show you the earth and snow and rain and all I have seen.

I'll show you the humid remains in my memory
And my mind that writes sonnets
For each memory I've ever had.

I'll show you the light and the dark and the mirage of this world in my palm.

And I'll show you the endless null resting in my hands.

I'll show you the last remnants of love within me,
Because by then,
Even I will be broken.

And I'll hope that you can tell me what it all means.

i mention fish twice

i am mesmerised
by the night.
it breathes life into me,
like a dead corpse
being reanimated in the afterlife.

like a fish learning to swim,
i come alive in ways
that are so natural,
so familiar to me.
i was born with the night
sinking into me,
flowing through me.

whenever i open my mouth
there is some remnant
of the midnight sky.

i write so often
about the wind on my skin
as i lie back on solid ground
and stare into the black chasm above
that threatens to swallow me up
if i stare any longer.

if only i could stay forever
here,
in this moment
where no one can see me
or hear me.
and even now
the clock has fallen asleep.

but these words are useless.
their cryptic meanings
i can never decipher,
and i never know how to use them

when i want to tell you
of what it's like inside my mind.

when i sit in a corner
and the words start to form
in my head,
i never know who i'm talking to.

i never know who
these poems are meant for.

maybe they'll find
who they were written for.

maybe they're written
just for you.

maybe they're written
for me.

when i sit there at night,
the feeling comes over me.
i can just about see
someone beside me,
and my hands start writing
to convey what i want to say.

without a thought,
the words roll off,
and i fill page after page.
i write for hours
about almost nothing,
caught in the conversation,
but unable to fluently converse.

i won't blame you
if you can't quite understand
what this poem is about.

i am watched

as i scribble
and draw.

when i am done
and the poem is finished,
i look down
at what i've written.

none of the words are mine
and not one of them
makes sense.

or at least that's how it seems.

and then i stare
out there
into that wicked night.

i am alone.

there is no one here besides me.

i can think.

for me
my happiness is hard earned.
yet
i'm always happy.

what a wicked night,
for me to sometimes become sad.

at times like this
i wish i knew how to write
a poem
that could actually
tell you how i feel.
i wish i could write of flowers
and how they curl up
when i touch them.

i wish i could tell you
that i have a fish
and when it looks at me
i don't know if it sees me
or just sees through me.
i want to hold it
i want to hug it
i want to show it i love it.

but that would kill it.

i wish i could describe
the look on my face
each morning,
when i look into the mirror
and realise
that the cruel dark sky
has somehow disappeared.

i wish i could show you
what this crooked night looks like
through my eyes.

This World

The sky was darkening
And the sun was slowly sinking in the sky
But still
It pained to look at it.

When I looked directly at it
My vision shook
And so I lowered my eyes.

Throughout the morphing sky
With hues of pale blue
A few desolate clouds
Hovered over me.

Almost golden,
The clouds sunk low
And I could almost taste them.

The air tasted of salt.

My eyes stung with salt.

I sat on the cold grass
Right where I could view
That glorious sea.

Beside the small hill I sat on
Ran a road
And perpendicular to the road sat a bridge.

A bridge over the entire ocean.
A bridge past where I could see.
A bridge to somewhere I had never been.

The busy cars and people
Walked past that very bridge,

But none walked across it.

I sat and watched over them.

The once still sea
Bubbled up and sprayed more salt
Into the heavy damp air.
My hair flew up
As it was pushed away from my face.

Like a constant hum
Of the hummingbird's heart,
The water thrashed and struggled.
Not just here
Where I sat,
But everywhere
Anywhere
The only sound anyone could really hear
Was the gentle ocean
Going about its day
As it always had
And always will.

The grass rustled in the wind
And my knees felt
The green blades dancing and pushing
Against me.

That wind carried and stirred up the sea.
The ocean grew just a little louder.

The sun was half swallowed
By that very sea of blue,
And its golden light
Had begun to touch the tips of the water.

I watched the gentle waves
Reflect the light.
The droplets thrown from the sea
Turned into a beautiful yellow

Before falling back and turning blue again.

Right past my knees and the grass
Ran a few small grasshoppers.
With long spindly legs
And their little green arms
They hopped
And hopped
And hopped,
Their antennae swishing in the breeze.

Behind them ran a few bunnies
Some white with brown spots
And some brown with white spots.
They ran from place to place
While jumping and rolling in the grass.

I smiled.

And then I heard a hum.
Not the ocean
But a real hummingbird
Hovered over a tree.

It moved fast
And then hovered
And then moved fast again.
It then stopped by the tree
And seemed to look at me.

I placed my hands into the grass
And rubbed them there
Feeling the sensation.
When I pulled my hands away
They were covered in dirt.
My knees were also dirty.

A low flying plane
Soared above my head.
The grasshoppers

Bunnies
And the hummingbird
All turned to watch the plane with me.

The plane was loud.
It was loud enough to make me forget
The sound of the sea
Even if I remembered it again
In just a second.

Back then
I was so scared
Of forgetting the sound of the sea.
I feared that if I didn't listen
Every minute
Every second
I would one day cease to hear it.

The plane passed by
As all things do
So the creatures went about their day
Forgetting about the plane
And its noise.

I didn't.
I kept watching for the plane
Until I couldn't see it anymore.

I kept watching and watching.
I tried to listen for it
But it was no longer there.

I looked at the ocean.
Someday
I would definitely cease to hear it.

Someday
I'd be gone.

Nothing

Is forever.

Someday the sun would settle
Into that very noisy sea
And I wouldn't be there for it.

I stood up.

The creatures turned to stare again
But this time
They stared at me.

For all the time
That I have been here
I had never stood up.

My feet were not used to walking
But still they dragged me forward.

I felt the grass crunch gently
Beneath my bare feet
With every step I took.
Again and again
Repeatedly
My weight crushed the green blades.

And then I had run out of grass
And hesitatingly
I stepped onto the
Asphalt road.
It prickled a little
And it was painful to walk on.

I found my feet
Moving faster.
Before I knew it I was running.

Past the road,
Onto the slim stretch of sand
And into the water.

With a loud splash
My foot landed ankle deep
In the ocean.

The water was cold.

I felt the water wash over me
Before receding
And running away.

Before I could move,
The water came back to me
And swallowed my foot again.

I looked into that water
And I understood
That I was already gone.

The water did not
Reflect my image.
I couldn't see my face
In its deep blue.

I sunk to my knees
And sat there
On the tip of the beach,
Beside the water.

I let myself be
Gently caressed
By its steady movement.

I found myself waist deep
And then just as quickly
The water ran away.

The sound was all around me.
The hum of the sea.
I felt it against me.

Death was not the bridge.
It was not the ocean.
It was not a journey.

It was not different
From the place of the living.
It was the same place
The same people
The same sights.

Death was the grassy hill.
It was the silence.

It was peaceful.

Death was the world
Finally holding me
And hugging me
And singing me to sleep.
It wasn't darkness.
It was the world closing my eyes
And telling me that finally
I could relax
And let go
Of anything
And everything.

BOOM!

With a startle
I open my eyes
And find myself still here,
Still alive.

If I ever die
It will be like that.
It will be like coming home
After a hard day.

I know it will be.

Because how could this world,
That I have loved with my heart,
Dare to make me unhappy
By sending me to a death I don't want?

How could this world,
That even now
Watches over me
With love,
Dare to someday leave me alone?

How could this world
Ever cease to love me?

How could this world
Ever forget me?

How could this world
Ever cease to be mine?

I know
It never will.
Some things
Can be forever.

Acknowledgements

First of all, I'd like to thank my little sister, Dhanishtta. She's been there for me throughout this journey and she's helped me whenever I was low. Dhanishtta, I love you so much. You're the best.

Thank you to my parents, Prasanna and Swarupa, for helping and supporting me not just in writing but in everything I do. I love you both.

A massive thank you to my friends Ananya, Isha, Jacinth, Jacob, Safa, Ummehani and Zainab for being with me every step of the way. I wouldn't have come this far without your encouragement and eagerness to help me. I owe you guys everything.

A special shout-out to Akkshaya for reading my work whenever she had free time. Your praise meant the world to me.

I'd also like to thank all the family and friends who have shown interest or appreciation for my writing throughout the years. Thank you to the teachers without whom I wouldn't know how to write.

If you've picked this book up and given it a read, thank you for taking the time to read my poetry.

Finally, thank you to my younger self, for persevering despite it all. Thank you, young Srika, for continuing to write. I love you.

www.ingramcontent.com/pod-product-compliance
Lightning Source LLC
LaVergne TN
LVHW041107150826
845673LV00007B/1956

9798891335264